The Gospel of Survival Skills

Survival Skills For Finding Your Way Through Tough Times

This Wisdom Is Based Upon The Teachings And Revelations of Jesus Christ!

Written By
Rev. Dr. Geraldine L. Johnson-Carter

"ANYTHING you can imagine for yourself is possible"

-Geri Johnson-Carter

© **Copyright 2022 by** The Door 2 Success Publishing **- All rights reserved.**

This document is geared towards providing exact and reliable information in regards to the topic and issue covered.

The publication is sold with the idea that the publisher is not required to render accounting, officially permitted, or otherwise, qualified services. If advice is necessary, legal or professional, a practiced individual in the profession should be ordered.

From a Declaration of Principles which was accepted and approved equally by a Committee of the American Bar Association and a Committee of Publishers and Associations.

In no way is it legal to reproduce, duplicate, or transmit any part of this document in either electronic means or in printed format. Recording of this publication is strictly prohibited and any storage of this document is not allowed unless with written permission from the publisher. All rights reserved.

The information provided herein is stated to be truthful and consistent, in that any liability, in terms of inattention or otherwise, by any usage or abuse of any policies, processes, or directions contained within is the solitary and utter responsibility of the recipient reader.

Under no circumstances will any legal responsibility or blame be held against the publisher for any reparation, damages, or monetary loss due to the information herein, either directly or indirectly.

Respective authors own all copyrights not held by the publisher. The information herein is offered for informational purposes solely, and is universal as so. The presentation of the information is without contract or any type of guarantee assurance.

The trademarks that are used are without any consent, and the publication of the trademark is without permission or backing by the trademark owner. All trademarks and brands within this book are for clarifying purposes only and are the owned by the owners themselves, not affiliated with this document.

Table Of Contents

My Prayer For You	8
There's Nothing Impossible To God	9
Don't Lose Hope	11
Everyone Wants To Be HAPPY!	13
Happiness Is An Inside Job And Your Only Job	18
Be Inner Directed	27
The Energy Of Thoughts	31
Detach From Outcomes	47
Manage Your Expectations	54
Be Grateful For Yourself	60
Be Present And Listen	64
Don't Complain	65
Practice Humility	67
Create Your Dream	69

Daily Personal Creeds   71

In Conclusion   78

My Prayer For You

Infinite Father, I know that all things are possible to "You". I know that, "You" have created me as a divine, perfect, spiritual being, made in Your image and likeness, which is perfect.

I now claim that perfection in body, mind, and spirit. I accept health, I give thanks for it, and I accept the manifestation of health in my body. And so it is.

"What things so ever ye desire, when ye pray believe that ye receive them and ye shall have them"

- Mark 11:24

There's Nothing Impossible To God

All things are possible to Him. The infinite Love of God is greater than any condition. God is working through the doctors and nurses to help me, but God is the real healer.

Of myself I do nothing. The Father within, he does the work. I AM a perfect, divine, spiritual being. My body is made of pure spiritual substance. I am one with God and God is one with me.

Right now the healing Presence of God is cleansing me, healing me of any seeming imperfection. God's infinite Love neutralizes all fear, uncertainty, all bitterness and un forgiveness.

God's love permeates every part of my life and my being. I am made whole and perfect now. I accept this perfect healing now. I thank God to whom this physical perfection is already known.

In the Mind of God I have never been less than perfect. Therefore his healing has already taken place in the Mind of God.

Don't Lose Hope

Every one of us has experienced times when we feel unhappy or unfulfilled. Sometimes we are not even sure why.

I have spent many years examining what it is that makes us unhappy, and how to change that feeling for good by using our own inner abilities.

Many of the strategies that I have developed were the result of trying things that did not work, and then looking deeper and trying again. Some were the result of my periods of sheer desperation.

What I have learned is that we all have the capacity within us to make our lives magnificent. When we're not satisfied we start to search for answers.

What is often frustrating is how long this can take. I hope this short book will shorten the amount of time it takes for you to find those answers.

Everyone Wants To Be HAPPY!

Everyone wants to be successful. We all want to feel safe, secure and in control of our destiny. We want to feel connected to each other and connected to the world around us.

Everyone wants to feel included. We know that there is power in unity. The goal of life is constant improvement. There is such beauty in the world.

Far too often we get so busy that we fail to notice the beauty and we fail to realize the potential that we possess.

Very often we see so much rage, anger and sadness while so many people are fearful and disillusioned. Far too many of us have become entangled in the pettiness of everyday life.

We lose hope in the everyday grind, the job, the commute, the problems, the bills, etc. We are so much more than that.

You must begin by knowing that everything will be fine. But you have to know it faithfully and not just believe it. You are in control of your life and in control of how you feel at all times.

All of us humans as a species, are still in our infancy. If the age of the Earth were compared to five miles of highway, we would be a fraction of an inch at the last part of that five miles.

We are still young, we have a lot to learn and that is fine. Our happiness and success or lack thereof, begins with our thoughts and the subsequent feelings and actions produced by those thoughts.

Those feelings and actions directly affect our daily mindset, the way that we relate to one another, and our attitude towards life perhaps more so than we ever realized.

The way that we relate to each other affects the way that we feel about our life tremendously. Happiness and joy is your natural state.

You were meant to be happy and successful to enjoy your time on earth. The following topics will provide you with some simple, yet effective ways of returning to back that natural state.

As well as suggestions to help you to become successful and adapt to any situation that you consider to be a problem. I have spent many years studying how to return to this natural state.

Within this small but mighty book I would like to share with you what I have learned throughout my lifetime of experiences. My hope is that it helps your life as it has mine.

Happiness Is An Inside Job And Your Only Job

Happiness and success are not outside you. They do not come about as the result of outside events. You alone are in charge of how you feel. You are the soul master of your emotions at all times.

It all begins with your thoughts. It's not the events of your life that determine how you feel. It's the way that you process those events through the filter of your thoughts.

Your lifelong happiness and abundant success in turn, improves the world around you for everyone. You may be wondering how is that so?

Whatever you focus your thoughts on and the subsequent actions produced by those thoughts, expand exponentially and affect everyone around you, especially those you love.

We know that we feel best when we are fair, when we are kind and we treat others with respect. We accomplish the greatest levels of success when our work benefits ourselves and others.

It's all ENERGY. Every thought and every action has energy within it. That energy is either high and positive or low and negative.

You can develop the skills to solve anything that you see as a problem and avoid the things that make you unhappy.

It is important to examine the way that we treat each other and how that affects everything else in our lives. Just start by learning to cope with the common traps that cause us pain and stress.

Let go of the past, recognize jealousy for what it is. Avoid conflict, comparison to others and the illusion of failure.

Find ways to make your personal relationships even more magnificent than you ever imagined possible by giving our loved ones respect and kindness.

Learn to create within yourself the daily reality that up until now you had only dreamed of. Find balance in your life by developing peaceful and fulfilling personal rituals.

Start by developing daily routines that you can enjoy every day. Discover, at last, your reason for being and your purpose for living.

Then start on the path toward happiness and all the success that you desire. This lifelong happiness is the achievement of success in any quantity that you desire and the concept of unity.

Feel yourself living in a world without exclusion that you can take part in bringing about by feeling connected to others at all times.

This act alone will make you feel included in the world and not excluded from the world. Success, happiness, abundance, peace and wealth is completely within your reach.

And you can learn how to attract it from others who have already. If you can see yourself being that or having that, you can also be it and have that you desire in your own life.

It's totally within your power. From this day forward, anything that you can imagine for yourself is possible. Start setting your sights high.

You were meant to be happy and successful. You were meant to experience a meaningful life with all of its abundance to enjoy your time on earth!

By far the most expansive force in the universe is a human being relentlessly pursuing their dream! Anything is possible. Anything! From now on, you must set your sights unreasonably high.

Highlight that and feel that in your mind and body. Isn't that a wonderful concept? It is also absolutely true.

Most of us have allowed ourselves to be conditioned to believe in what is not possible, instead of what is truly possible with faith and action.

Today you will discover how to let go of that belief. You will learn what shared qualities that extraordinary, happy and highly successful people possess.

It's not necessarily special talent or a high IQ. It's a drive and desire that comes from being passionate about what they do and what they want to attract into their life.

They love what they do and it shows. How does a person get that drive and desire? How do they keep it? By finding passion and purpose for the people they love outside of themselves.

It comes from within and it never goes away, no matter what happens. It's born out of passion and they have no concept of failure. Failure does not exists for them.

Of course they are disappointed by setbacks, just like everyone else. The difference is that they understand that setbacks are just part of the process.

They're not destroyed by setbacks, they learn from them. You must begin by changing your concept of what's possible. You accomplish this by becoming "INNER DIRECTED."

Be Inner Directed

This means that your concept of what's possible for you comes from your own thoughts and is completely independent of what others believe is possible for you.

You will need to be completely unreasonable in your expectations. Michelangelo said, "The greater danger is not our hopes are too high and we don't reach them, it's that they are too low and we do."

There is nothing in the universe that cannot be achieved once you are able to form a clear picture in your mind and begin to act with passion on that picture.

In Proverbs it clearly reads: "As a man thinketh in his heart, so is he." There was a time when you knew and believed that anything was possible.

Think back to when you were a child. You had no doubt that anything that you could imagine could become real. It all begins with your thoughts and what you think about all day.

What you think about every day expands exponentially. Every single thing that is now in your life was once just a thought you told the universe that you wanted.

This works for your positive thoughts and your negative ones also. Undoubtedly, there were times in your life when you felt like you absolutely had to have something and then you got it!

That thought was for a relationship, a job, a home or anything else and you were able to attract that desire into your life because you formed a clear picture in your mind.

Then you began to act on that pictured desire consciously and unconsciously. Your thoughts become things when you desire them strong enough and when they are fueled with emotions.

William James, a Psychologist and medical doctor has been called the father of modern psychology, discovered a universal law which states:

"If you can form a clear picture in your mind of what you want to attract or become and hold it there, it has to happen." It will always materialize.

This is true because when you focus your thoughts on anything long enough, you begin to act on those thoughts until they become a reality.

The Energy Of Thoughts

Every single thought that goes through your mind all day produces energy. The energy of your thoughts will dramatically affect the way that you feel and the way that you act.

The energy of your thoughts is either high and positive, or low and negative. High energy thoughts are of gratitude, appreciation, love, kindness, respect and empathy just to name a few.

The energy of these thoughts are positive, so they have a positive effect on you, how you feel and how you feel about everyone around you.

Low energy thoughts are thoughts of anger, shame, violence, fear and doubt. They have a negative effect on you, your body and everyone that you come in contact with.

Have you ever noticed that there are certain people that you just feel better around? Their energy is positive, and you can sense this. In general these people are pleasant, kind and encouraging.

They are usually cheerful and show enthusiasm and genuine interest in others. Have you ever had the opposite experience? There are people who make you feel worse when they're close to you.

They are usually very negative, sad, angry and unhappy. They are down and often in a state of internal and external conflict more than not.

If you want your life to become magnificent, it is critical to maintain the energy of your thoughts. You accomplish this by becoming very careful about what thoughts you accept in your mind.

A clear mental picture of what you want to attract, plus the positive energy of your daily thoughts is the key.

This picture is what will expand in your life if you can keep it there and begin to act on those images. We literally become our thoughts.

It is not the events of your life that affect how you feel, it's what you expect for yourself and what you are willing to attempt to accomplish that creates a joyful and peaceful life.

It's how you process these events through the filter of your thoughts. Everything in the universe is connected because everything created shared and still shares the same source.

It makes no difference what you call it. It has been called God, Source, Higher Power, Creator, Universal Energy, and many other names.

I respect whatever you call it. This is not about religion. It is the same intelligence that created everything. A spiritual approach would be to call it our Higher Power.

This Higher Power is everywhere. It is an energy that is in everyone and part of everything. Everything and everyone is connected by it.

What is wonderful is that since you are part of the universe, and everything in the universe is connected, you are also connected to this Higher Power.

And you are also therefore connected to everyone else, as well as connected to whatever it is that you want to attract in your life.

What you want is not "out there" somewhere, it is everywhere, and therefore it is within you, or at least within your reach. In other words, what you want also wants you!

You have within you, right now, the ability to attract anything that you want for yourself. Your job is to know and be clear as to what it is that you really want and why you want it.

You have to trust for now that you wouldn't have been given the desire to want it, without having the ability to attract it. By keeping a clear picture in your mind, you will begin to act upon that image.

That action will pull you toward what you want. In order to succeed in any area of your life, in personal relationships, in business or anything else you want, it takes energy and passion combined.

And it takes the ability to see yourself already doing it or having it in your life. Decide exactly what you want in your life and begin to act as though it is already real for you.

And I promise that before long, it will be. Have you ever met a happy, successful person who didn't have energy and passion? Every successful person has an abundance of both.

They also have a clear mental picture of what they want. You've had it too, on many occasions, I'm sure! Everyone has.

Think back to an experience when you did something so well that you surprised yourself.

Something that you doubted could even be possible until it came.

Maybe it was a presentation that you made as a gift for a loved one, or something that you wrote, or a race that you won.

Whatever it was, I'm sure that you were passionate about it. You also saw yourself doing it. What was going through your mind when you accomplished it?

You were able to focus your thoughts, your energy, your passion, and you saw yourself doing it. This caused you to act upon what you were seeing.

Your thoughts are what made everything that you accomplished possible. But those thoughts can just as easily make things impossible, so you have to be very careful.

Your thoughts are the resources that you use to purchase everything that you want in life, but they can also be used to purchase what you don't want.

What I mean is whatever you focus your thoughts on will become what you expect. What is your daily inner dialogue like? Are most of your thoughts happy and cheerful?

Do you feel grateful for the abundance that you already possess? Or do you find that you are often sad, overwhelmed or agitated?

Are your thoughts on what you don't like, or don't want? If your thoughts are always on what you don't want or what has always happened in the past, that is exactly what you will continue to get.

For example, if you would like to attract more abundance into your life, it is not possible to do so if all day long your thoughts are on how little you have or a constant fear that there is not enough.

You cannot attract the relationship of your dreams if all day long you are thinking about how bad you look, or if you are feeling in some way inadequate or unworthy.

Your thoughts must be on what you want to attract into your life with passion. Let's say you would really love to have abundance show up in your life. Abundance in the universe is unlimited.

There is an infinite supply of everything. It is all around you. Other people have it, why can't you? Unlimited abundance is available to everyone but you have to feel worthy of it.

If it's available to everyone, then it is also available to you. You can use a tanker to fill yours up or you can use a paper cup. It's entirely up to you. It all depends on your thoughts.

If you believe that the amount of abundance that you deserve or can attract is limited in some way, you will act on those thoughts and create a limited amount of abundance for yourself and your family.

If your thoughts are of scarcity and you are regularly concerned that there will not be enough, you will attract scarcity and for sure, there will never be enough.

You really do attract back whatever energy that you put out. This is how the law of universal energy works for everyone.

If the energy that you put out is always high and positive, you will do better in business, better in relationships and everything else that is important to you.

You may be wondering how do you keep your energy high and stay careful as to what you take into your mind?

Realize that everything has energy, and that energy affects the way that you feel. Start by being more cautious about how much negative news that you watch.

Pay close attention to what you read, who you put yourself around and what you watch on television. We are bombarded with media in our modern world and a great deal of it is negative.

Do not close yourself out from the world and do stay informed, but limit negative media. Then practice feeding your mind with positive influences.

Positive influences such as positive and relaxing music or positive youtube videos. Try to watch programs that are positive and uplifting and contain a minimum amount of violence.

Detach From Outcomes

You will always do your best when you are able to be detached from the outcomes of life. When you're able to live in harmony with life and cooperating with the flows of life without fighting.

When you are truly genuine and sincere with others and not after personal gain. When you are selfless and not selfish, it all just seems to flow.

Maslow suggests that human beings are inherently good not evil. This is absolutely true. We want to good because it makes us feel good about ourselves in the process.

He also believed that once a persons basic needs are met such as food, clothing, shelter and security, we are then free to become the best person we can be. (self actualized)

Our main motivation for a chosen endeavor should be for the fulfillment and contribution to others. Our actions should be motivated by the fulfillment of ourselves through the fulfillment of others.

If we are attached to the outcomes in the lives of others, we are in a state of wanting. This puts us out of balance because we are focused on the scarcity in others lives and not the abundance.

Our giving should be out of pure love and the wanting to see others do well, but we are only responsible for our positive input, not the outcome. They must want their own outcome.

You give away your power when you become attached to the outcome of a situation which is beyond your control. So, how do you "detach" from the outcome?

The only way to detach from the outcome is by overcoming fear and doubt. You must have confidence and faith in your own value and your abilities for attracting into your life what you want.

You must know that you are worthy of what you want, just as they must know the same to get what they want from life. When you are detached from the outcome, you are in balance with your desires.

Your desires then become your choices. You will be at your best and most confident. Detachment means that your actions flow out of your love and your passion for the service to others.

Your actions must always be in the best interest of the targeted population that you will serve, not your own selfish self interest.

It is best to tell no one of your plans. Keep them private, they are yours and yours alone. Resist the temptation to share them with anyone.

This way you will never have to defend them or explain your reasons or your capabilities. You do this in order to avoid negative feed back, which will only cause you to doubt your abilities.

Imagine yourself with an imaginative force field around you, like a protective bubble. Inside your force field is a safe and fertile place for your desires to expand into your reality.

On the outside are all the negative thoughts, all your doubts about your ability and any other negative thoughts or comments others may have about your plans.

Leave the negative energy on the outside and always keep an open mind! An open mind is the only mind that can learn and expand. An open mind is creative and free to flow.

An open mind can advance, grow and improve. You should be open to everything but not certain of anything.

Everything in the universe is either growing or dying out. That which serves a purpose continues to grow.

That which no longer serves a purpose, either dies off or becomes obsolete. You must make the conscious decision to grow and expand so anything in your life is possible!

Manage Your Expectations

We must learn to accept temporary setbacks and disappointments at all times because these are a normal part of the process of improvement. Have faith.

Faith is knowing that something is true without needing proof. You must have faith in your abilities. Faith is the only antidote to your fear.

It is only fear that causes you to doubt what is possible for you. It is fear that keeps you from attaining what you want from life.

It is important to develop a new way of thinking which empowers you, instead of holding you back. Faith is a choice. You must choose to adopt it.

Faith comes from trusting that you are part of an intelligent system. A system that is guided by a Higher Power to which you are connected to at all times.

Faith is the ability to trust that any past experience that you have lived through has brought you here to where you are today. And every bit of it had to happen to be who you are and where you are!

Whether it feels like it or not, trust that you are better for the experience. Everything that has ever happened to you has prepared you to move forward.

You have to make a conscious decision to have faith and know that anything that you can see for yourself in your life is possible.

Faith is like a super power. Once you make the decision to have faith, you can have the ability right now to attract anything that you desire into your life.

You will need faith to do anything you want to do! Anything in the whole world can be yours if you trust God and you have unshakeable faith!

STEP 1: Get started on something that you have been wanting to try. Something you may have felt that you didn't have the ability to accomplish.

Work at keeping the energy of your thoughts high and positive by monitoring what kind of information you consume and the influences you allow in.

Limit your exposure to anything and anyone negative. Anything you can do to get you closer to your dream, begin it today. Don't put it off until tomorrow. Boldness has genius, power and magic in it." - Johann Wolfgang Von Goethe

"Gratitude is not only the greatest of virtues, but the parent of all others. " - *Cicero*

STEP 2: Develop an attitude of gratitude, appreciation, and humility. Life is a miracle. To be born is a true gift out of the many who do not make it to life.

Once you realize that you already possess everything that you need in life and your potential to achieve anything that you want, you will begin to feel abundantly grateful for the gift of life.

It is impossible to experience fear and doubt while you are grateful. You should have all the abundance that you want, all you have to do is take a step towards it everyday.

Be Grateful For Yourself

Be thankful for your body. It is truly a miracle made up of multiple complex systems. These systems work together day and night in perfect harmony and complex cooperation.

Be thankful for your mind. The human mind is incomparable to any other force that we know of in the universe. It is our direct link to our Creator.

We are miraculous creatures that possess the ability to think deeply and critically. Our thoughts make us who we are. Our thoughts last forever.

Be thankful for the ability to adjust and make decisions. We have the ability to co-create into reality whatever we desire and act upon.

Be thankful for the infinite abundance that you already possess. Spend some time in wonder and appreciation of the miracles all around you. Be thankful for the here and now in this moment.

It is all we have. The past is gone and the future is not guaranteed to any one of us. Right here and now this moment is everything. Gratitude is being happy with what you have.

It is also the prerequisite to having more come into your life. Abundance is a state of mind and it is fluid. When you are truly grateful for your life, more abundance will always flow to you.

You can be rich now, today. You can never be poor if you are grateful for what you have. The choice is yours. Live in a constant state of gratitude and wonder. All abundance flows to you from there.

Be grateful for your relationships. Be thankful for your family and all the people who care about you. Every good relationship that you enjoy enhances your experience of life.

Let the people you love know how much you appreciate them. They need to hear it. It fills them up with the joy and love that we all deserve.

Be Present And Listen

When you are with someone, be fully present. Nothing lets someone know that they are appreciated better than your being present in the conversation and paying full attention to them.

Try not to be on your phone or thinking about something else. Be present and really listen. When someone is speaking to you, try not to think about what you want to say next. Be genuine and real.

Don't Complain

Never take anything for granted. At times, we all go about in pity for ourselves. Our minor problems and inconveniences seem so difficult and serious sometimes that we allow them to get us down.

Focus on the abundance and good fortune that we already possess. We are being guided by a Higher Power. This Higher Power is the energy that keeps us healthy and strong.

Not complaining allows us to prosper and enjoy abundance even while things are tough. Always count the blessings that you already possess by being grateful and focused on what you do have.

Practice Humility

The goal of life is constant learning and improvement. Keep and open mind and develop a love for learning. Don't ever become an "expert" who knows it all about everything.

Be humble and appreciate all of the knowledge and wisdom that you do have. And allow others to feel comfortable to express information that you may already know.

Let others shine and show their light. By always talking about how much you know and not allowing others to express what they know also, will cause people will shut down around you.

We are all special and worthy of listening to, even if its repetitive. Everyone wants to feel heard and approved of.

Just by listening to someone talk without interruption, instead of always needing to talking is an easy way to make someone feel important and special.

Create Your Dream

"The true meaning of life is to find your gift. The purpose of life is to give it away!" - Pablo Picasso

Every one of us has a dream which is simply a vision of our best life. Every moment we patiently wait for it to arrive. We wait for the conditions to be just right, but that can take forever.

That is why you cannot wait for the perfect time to act on your dream to arrive. You must create your dream. Are you willing to do whatever it takes to make your dream your daily reality?

This is where the human mind connects to divinity. This is where creation takes place, this is where we have to push ourselves past what our minds thought was possible.

Happiness, success, wealth and abundance is not reserved for "other people." It is for everyone including you. The human mind is a miracle and its possibilities are endless.

Daily Personal Creeds

The following daily creeds will help you gain health, wealth, faith, a deeper connection to God and peace of mind:

- The human experience can be wonderful. Along with pain can come joy, peace and hope! Live your life on purpose and to the fullest

- I believe in God the source of creative energy in the universe and in me

- I believe that the spirit of God was placed in my body

- I was sent to earth to understand and do God's will

- I believe that a major part of my purpose is to always treat other's like I would want them to treat me

- I believe that God will lend me everything I need to complete the tasks that I'm assigned

- I believe that God will supply the necessary co worker with similar values to help me accomplish my assignments

- I believe that my family is my God given circle of support and caring while I am functioning on this frequency

- I believe in prayer and meditation. They are my tools to keep in touch with the divine energy and I will respond to its direction

- I believe that my attitude, behavior and my choices promote peace in my life and I take the responsibility for securing my own peace

- I believe that when my work is finished, God will call my spirit back to join the divine energy and I will leave this frequency and this body behind in peace

- I believe in God who has been revealed through the physical in the life of Jesus Christ

- I believe that God's will is to be known by me and thus comes to me, calls me and changes me

- I believe God knows all there is to know about me, but loves me in spite of my sin, ambiguity and confusion

- I believe God has a purpose for my life and has chosen me, sustained me and directs me and will continue to make my life path clear to me

- I believe God will abide with me and will provide me companions for my journey

- I have everything I need to experience Bliss in my life

- I believe God entered my consciousness in a new form and has awakened my interests and concerns

- All things work for the good of those who love the Lord!

- What you believe you can conceive, what you can conceive, you can achieve!

- Any bridge is good that takes you over the stream

- Things are a part of your life situation, they are not your whole life

- Secret to confronting anything in any situation in life is to stand and take one step at a time

- Count your blessings!

- Watch what you ask for, because you just might get it!

- A person who loves music, who loves art, respects the spirit world and thinks with their heart is pure

- Forget and forgive what has passed and let God handle the future

- Adversity is the greatest teacher

- Life is a game and there are rules for living

- My perception is powerful and I can decide if what happens in my life helps me or hinders me

In Conclusion

Shakespeare said, "All the world's a stage" In the stage play of your life, your spirit is the leading actor.

This body and mind serve as props but neither the mind nor the body can play the staring role. This is because your spirit is what completes you.

Only your spirit can bring passion to your role in the world. The joy is in the journey and not the destination.

We all need a safe place to repair the broken Spirit. A safe place of peace to get out of your mind and into your heart. All lasting healing begins within.

In order to maintain wellness you must take care of your whole self by giving proper care and attention not only to your body, but to your spirit and mind as well.

Before you can enjoy lasting results in the outer world, you must restore proper faith, peace and balance to your inner world.

You have the inborn capacity for internal and external life balance. Internalize simple life principles that help you understand who you are.

Remember that the spirit is the real you. Your spirit is the part of you that gives meaning to life. It represents your pure and true personal destiny.

MAY GOD BLESS YOU!

"And we know that for those who love God all things work together for the good of those who love him, and who have been called according to his purpose."

-Romans 8:28

NOTES

Made in the USA
Monee, IL
26 September 2022

14682271R00046